"And you wonder, Herman, why I never want to go to Italian restaurants!"

by Jim Unger

Andrews and McMeel, Inc.

A Universal Press Syndicate Company
Kansas City

First printing, March 1977
Second printing, March 1979

"Herman" is syndicated internationally by
UNIVERSAL PRESS SYNDICATE

Copyright © 1977 by

UNIVERSAL PRESS SYNDICATE
Published simultaneously in Canada by Gage Publishing.

ISBN: 0-8362-0702-5

Library of Congress Catalog Card Number: 77-71686

"You're not Robert Redford."

"We'll take you off the vitamins for
a couple of days."

"Well, now we know what all that noise was
about last night."

"This one's not signed."

"Members of the jury, have you reached a verdict?"

"I'll come back later when you're not busy."

"Will you quit arguing and give me my seven iron."

"Couldn't resist, could you?"

"Your mother warned me you'd start complaining about your food."

"I thought you said you were coming home
next Sunday"

"Is there anything you need before I go?"

"It's the cook's coffee-break, so eat your dessert first."

"Try to guess who this is for..."

"ONE."

"Is that your idea of 20 pounds of potatoes?"

"34-24-36...It sounds like your right arm."

"Sure, I'd love a second honeymoon...who with?"

"Want me to wrap it?"

"Sorry to keep you both waiting out here. Where's your wife?"

"Whaddya making?"

"Want mashed potatoes?"

"If I've gotta do typing and stuff like that, I want more money!"

"Get up, you idiot. When I say, 'how do you plead?'
I wanna know if you're 'guilty' or 'not guilty'."

"How much longer did he tell you to stay on this banana diet?"

"That new guy was supposed to be helping me roll this."

"Haven't you got a brush?"

"I know you're in bed with the flu, but I need the
keys to the filing cabinet."

"Your four aces don't beat my two eights unless
you've got a red king!"

"Think it'll work?"

"Try to relax."

"You're supposed to say 'I do' not 'I'll try.'"

"Did you sleep okay, Herman?"

"Your mother said you loved eggs for breakfast!"

"Listen, I gotta go. There's a guy waiting to
use the phone."

"All I said was I didn't want it in stereo."

"Two of these just fell out of the car."

"Did he make you buy anything?"

"'One Hundred and One Ways to Rip Off Credit
Companies'... is that cash or charge?"

"I make it a rule never to lend money to people who borrow!"

"What song did you sing?"

"Had any luck?"

"Don't forget to lock up when you leave, Henderson."

"I'd expect it from the younger generation, but
asking for more money at your age is
absolutely inexcusable."

"Can I take them with water?"

"I was in the neighborhood and I thought I'd drop
in for a couple of weeks."

"It comes with a guarantee for five years or until you use it, whichever comes first."

"I'll work my way up your arm and you tell
me when you feel anything."

"Is that the only way you can have a good time,
smashing up public property?"

"Show me that piece of paper again with the
calculations on it."

"The man we're looking for will be dynamic and aggressive."

"Three nights in a row I've dreamt
you were Dracula."

"Is that the tie I bought him for Christmas?"

"Do I get that one again?"

"He loves a cup of tea."

"Shall I turn it off?"

"I read somewhere that expensive champagne
doesn't go 'pop.'"

"I don't care if it is plastic. I could have had
a heart attack."

"Night work! You mean when it's dark?"

"Have you got any others with more spikes?"

"The sporting goods store phoned. You left your hat
on the counter."

"Madam, giving your husband 'twenty years in the slammer' is not my idea of a divorce settlement."

"STAMPEDE!"

"Why don't you start climbing out and I'll keep
trying the buttons."

"I'm your anesthetist and he's my 'back-up man'."

"Stay calm...I'm gonna get a second opinion on your blood pressure."

"Sure it's big, but it'll do an average room in
three minutes."

"Your wife took the new baby home in a cab
an hour ago."

"You're certainly enjoying my little cakes. Have
another one!"

"Hold it! They're out of season."

"I take it you don't want any of this cheese."

"I'll only be gone for a month, so don't use the kitchen."

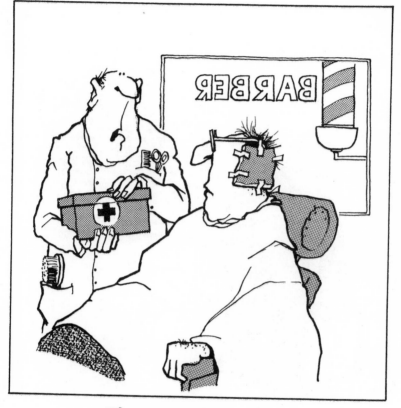

"There goes my tip, right?"

"Members of the jury, I ask you—does my client
look like a man of violence?"

"Wanna see the list of optional extras?"

"Your plane's been delayed ten minutes. A
couple of rivets popped loose."

"Here, you wanted a shark's-tooth necklace.
Dig those outa my leg."

OTHER POPULAR CARTOON COLLECTIONS FROM ANDREWS AND McMEEL

"Apart from a Little Dampness, Herman, How's Everything Else?"
By Jim Unger $2.45

And I'm Tank McNamara with the Norts Spews
By Jeff Millar and Bill Hinds $2.25

God Intended Blond Boys To Be Quarterbacks
By Jeff Millar and Bill Hinds $1.95

Life Is Just a Bunch of Ziggys
By Tom Wilson $1.95

It's a Ziggy World
By Tom Wilson $1.95

Never Get Too Personally Involved With Your Own Life
By Tom Wilson $1.95

Ziggys of the World Unite!
By Tom Wilson $1.95

Plants Are Some of My Favorite People
By Tom Wilson $1.95

Doonesbury: The Original Yale Cartoons
By Garry B. Trudeau $2.25

If you are unable to obtain these books from your bookseller, they may be ordered from the publisher. Enclose payment with your order.

Andrews and McMeel, Inc.

6700 Squibb Road
Mission, Kansas 66202